The Adventure in Dino Land

While every precaution has been taken in the preparation of this book, the publisher assumes no responsibility for errors or omissions, or for damages resulting from the use of the information contained herein.

ADVENTURE IN DINO LAND

First edition. March 14, 2023.

Copyright © 2023 Liom Liom.

ISBN: 979-8215900772

Written by Liom Liom.

The first day in Dino Land

It was a sunny day in Dino Land. Pino, a little dinosaur, had just hatched from his egg and was looking around curiously. He couldn't believe that he was finally in Dino Land, which he had only known from stories.

Pino was excited and a little scared at the same time, because he didn't know what to expect here. But he didn't have time to think about it, because suddenly he heard a loud roar. He looked around and discovered a big Triceratops staring at him.

Pino wanted to run away, but his little legs didn't carry him fast enough. The Triceratops came closer and Pino closed his eyes so he wouldn't have to see what was about to happen. But instead of an attack, Pino suddenly heard a voice.

"Hey little friend, are you lost?"

Pino opened his eyes and saw another dinosaur looking at him in a friendly way. The dino introduced himself as Timo and explained to Pino that he had landed in Dino Land, a place full of adventure and danger, but also full of friendship and fun.

Pino was relieved and curious at the same time. Timo offered to take him on a tour of Dino Land. Pino agreed enthusiastically and off the adventure went.

Timo led Pino through the forest, showed him the volcano and the lake where the dinos cooled off. Pino was fascinated by all the animals he saw. There were herbivores and carnivores, small and big dinos, those with long tails and those with spiky backs.

But suddenly they heard a loud rumbling sound. Timo explained to Pino that it was a landslide and they had to run away quickly. Pino felt his heart racing and his legs shaking. But Timo gave him courage and together they ran as fast as they could.

At the end of the tour, Pino was tired but also happy. He had learned so much and made so many new friends. He realized that there were many dangers in Dino Land, but that there were also many good things.

That people had to help each other and that friendship and cohesion were important.

Pino returned to his nest and fell into a deep sleep, exhausted but content. He knew that he would have many more adventures in Dino Land in the days and weeks to come, but he was ready for them. With his new friends by his side, he would be able to overcome any challenge.

Pino gets to know his dino friends

Pino woke up on a sunny morning and decided to go in search of friends. He knew there were many other dinosaurs in Dino Land, and he was eager to make new friends. So, he set out to meet the other dinos.

First, he met a friendly stegosaurus named Sammy. Sammy had lots of sharp thorns on his back, but he was very nice and invited Pino to a picnic. They shared their food and exchanged stories.

As they were eating, they suddenly heard a loud roar. Sammy explained that it was a Tyrannosaurus Rex, one of the most dangerous carnivores in Dino Land. Pino was scared, but Sammy calmed him down and told him not to worry as long as he was with him.

When the T-Rex came closer, Sammy bravely stood in front of Pino and showed him how to defend himself. He told him that it was important not to run away, but to be brave and defend yourself when you are attacked.

The T-Rex came closer and tried to attack Pino. But Sammy fought him off and defended Pino. The T-Rex finally gave up and walked away.

Pino was impressed by Sammy's courage and ability to protect him. He knew he had found a true friend. They played together all day and had a lot of fun.

At the end of the day, Pino met another dinosaur named Mia, a velociraptor. She was not as friendly as Sammy and Pino was afraid of her. But Sammy explained to him that they were not all friendly dinosaurs and that you always had to be careful.

Pino realized that it was important to be careful, but that you should also be open to making new friends. He had made not one, but two new friends that day who helped him explore and understand Dino Land.

The most important thing he had learned that day was that friendship and courage were very important in Dino Land. You had to be careful, but also be open to new experiences and friends. With his new friends by his side, Pino felt brave and ready for all the adventures that lay ahead.

A TRIP TO THE VOLCANO

Pino and his friends Sammy and Mia had decided to take a trip to the volcano. They had heard a lot about it and were curious to see what they would discover there. So they packed their backpacks and set off.

As they got closer, they could feel the heat and smell the smoke. It was an exciting feeling because they had never seen a volcano before. When they finally arrived, they were amazed at how big and powerful the volcano looked.

Pino and his friends decided to explore the volcano. They climbed over rocks and meandered through the lava flowing down the mountain. It was dangerous, but also exciting, and they all had a lot of fun.

Suddenly, they heard a loud rumbling. It was coming from inside the volcano. Pino and his friends got scared and wondered what was going to happen. Then they saw lava splashing out of the crater and flowing over the sides of the mountain.

Pino and his friends ran as fast as they could to get to safety. They could hear the thunder and crash of the volcano as they hurriedly moved away.

When they were finally safe, they took a deep breath. They were glad they had escaped the volcano and thanked Sammy for guiding them through the dangers.

They realized that you always have to be careful if you want to have adventures. You have to know how to behave in dangerous situations and that you should always be alert. But it was also important to know that you can rely on your friends and that together you are strong.

Pino and his friends returned with a new appreciation for adventure, aware that life can be full of challenges and dangers. But with the right attitude and the right friends by their side, they were able to overcome any obstacle and have exciting new experiences.

PINO AND THE STEGOSAURUS quarrel

One day, Pino met a stegosaurus named Spike on his way to the river. Pino and Spike talked for a while and found out that they had many interests in common. They decided to become friends and spent the whole day playing together.

But the next day, when Pino went back to the river, he saw Spike arguing with another dino. Pino approached and realized that it was a triceratops. Spike and the Triceratops had gotten into an argument over something small and just wouldn't listen to each other.

Pino decided to step in and settle the dispute. He tried to understand both sides and showed them that they had a lot in common. After a while they stopped arguing and were able to find a solution that was acceptable to both sides.

Spike and the Triceratops realized that they shouldn't fight over a small thing and that it was better to have fun together and be friends. They apologized to each other and agreed not to have any more fights in the future.

Pino had shown that one should always try to find a peaceful solution when there is an argument. He had also shown how important it is to make friends and maintain them instead of fighting over small things.

Pino and Spike became best friends and played together every day by the river. They knew they could always count on each other and that their friendship was much more important than any disagreement or argument they might have.

THE HUNT FOR THE LOST egg

One day Pino and his dinosaur friends noticed that a dinosaur egg had disappeared. They were worried because the egg belonged to a sad Mama Dino who didn't know where her baby had gone.

Pino and his friends decided to look for the egg and bring it back before it was too late. They knew they had to act fast to save the baby dino. They went off and searched everywhere in Dino Land.

Finally, they found a trail that led to the nest of a raptor. They were sure that the raptor had stolen the egg and hidden it in its nest. Pino and his friends decided to disguise themselves and carefully sneak up to the nest to get the egg back.

But the raptor was smart and noticed the dinos approaching his nest. He started chasing them and they had to act quickly to escape. However, Pino had an idea. He lured the raptor away while his friends stole the egg and brought it back to the Mama Dino.

Mama Dino was so relieved and happy to have her baby Dino back with her. She thanked Pino and his friends for their bravery and courage in retrieving the egg. Pino and his friends were proud to have helped and knew they had done a good deed.

The moral of this story was that it is important to help others and stand up for others, especially when they are sad or in trouble. It also shows the importance of working together and supporting each other to accomplish a common task. Pino and his friends had proven that they were strong and brave, and that they were willing to fight for the good of others.

A MYSTERIOUS RIDDLE

One day, Pino found a mysterious treasure map in Dino Land. He was excited and curious about what it could mean. Pino and his friends took a closer look at the map and noticed that it led to a hidden place where a mysterious riddle had to be solved.

The friends decided to work together to solve the riddle and find the treasure. They followed the map and finally came to a big tree in Dino Land. There was a cave there that they had to enter. But the cave was dark and scary, and they didn't know what to expect.

As they moved further into the cave, they noticed that there was a series of tasks that they had to solve. It was a difficult puzzle, but Pino and his friends worked hard together and helped each other to solve it. Finally, they found the treasure, which was made of sparkling gems and glittering gold.

But the treasure was not the most important thing for Pino and his friends. They were proud of the fact that they worked together and solved the puzzle. They learned that sometimes you have to work together and use the strengths of others to achieve a goal.

The moral of this story is that sometimes you face challenges that can only be solved if you work together and support each other. Pino and his friends proved that through teamwork and cohesion, you are able to overcome difficult tasks. And if you work hard, you can even find a treasure in the end.

PINO BECOMES A DETECTIVE

Pino and his friends were out and about in Dino Land when they suddenly noticed that something strange was going on. Some of the dinos in the land were mysteriously disappearing and no one knew where they had gone. Pino was curious and wanted to find out what had happened. So he decided to make himself a detective and solve the case.

Pino asked his friends if they would help him find the missing dinos. They immediately joined in and supported him in his search. Pino was sure that he would find the dinos if he just looked hard enough.

Pino and his friends began collecting clues and following tracks. They questioned other dinos in the country and looked around carefully. Finally, one clue led them to a hidden place where they discovered a dino being held captive.

Pino and his friends were relieved to have found the missing dino. They freed him and brought him back to his family. But they also knew that there were more dinos that had disappeared. So they continued their search and followed more tracks.

Finally, they discovered a secret cave where the missing dinos were being held. It was a trap set by an evil dino who had captured them. Pino and his friends fought bravely against the evil dino and managed to free the captured dinos.

In the end, all the dinos were saved and Pino and his friends had solved the case. They had proven that they were good detectives who were able to accomplish difficult tasks. They had also learned that if you really want to accomplish a thing, you should never give up.

The moral of this story is that if you work hard and don't get discouraged, you are able to accomplish difficult tasks. Pino and his friends had proven that through teamwork and determination, one is able to overcome even the most difficult challenges.

THE CASE OF THE MISSING bones

Pino and his friends were out and about in Dino Land when they suddenly noticed that something was wrong. The bones of some of the dinos in the land were mysteriously disappearing, and no one knew who was behind it. Pino and his friends were determined to solve the case and find the thief.

Pino began collecting clues and following up on leads. He questioned other dinos in the country and looked around carefully. Finally, one clue led him to a hidden place where he discovered a suspicious dino with bones in his possession.

Pino and his friends decided to set a trap to catch the thief. They pretended that they had found a new, valuable bone and waited for the thief to strike. Finally, the suspicious dinosaur came and tried to steal the bone. Pino and his friends struck and caught him.

When they questioned the thief, he confessed that he had stolen the bones to sell them to gain an advantage. Pino and his friends were disappointed that someone in Dino Land could be so mean.

They decided to turn the thief over to the dino community and hold him accountable for what he had done. The thief realized his mistake and apologized to the dinos in the land.

In the end, all the bones were returned and the thief was punished. Pino and his friends had solved the case and proved that they were good detectives. They had also learned that one should always tell the truth and act fairly.

The moral of this story is that you should be honest and act fairly. Pino and his friends had proven that it is wrong to steal and cheat others. They had also shown that through determination and teamwork, one is able to solve difficult problems.

THE GREAT DINO RACE

Pino and his friends had heard about a big dino race that would soon take place in Dino Land. They decided to participate and compete against other dinos.

They trained hard and prepared for the race. On the day of the race, they were ready and excited to compete against the other dinos. The race was tough and challenging, but Pino and his friends fought bravely and finally reached the finish line.

As they were celebrating their victory, they noticed that one of their opponents was lying on the ground injured. Pino and his friends decided to help him and take care of him instead of celebrating the victory.

They took care of the injured Dino and helped him get back on his feet. Even though they had won the race, they realized that it was more important to help others and be caring.

The Great Dino Race had shown them that it was important to be fair and sporting, but also to be there for others when they needed help.

Pino and his friends had proven that you should fight not only for your own success, but also for the well-being of others.

The moral of this story is that it is important to be fair and sportsmanlike, but also to be there for others when they need help. Pino and his friends had learned that there was more to life than winning. It was about being there for each other and helping each other.

PINO AS A RACER

Pino was a bright little dinosaur who had always dreamed of becoming a race car driver. One day he had the opportunity to participate in a race and make his dream come true.

Pino was thrilled and immediately started training. He practiced for hours to become faster and improve his skills. His friends watched him train and supported him.

When the day of the race finally came, Pino was ready. He stood at the starting line ready to compete against the other racers. The starting gun went off and Pino zoomed away.

The race was tough and challenging, but Pino fought bravely and gave it his all. He overtook his competitors and rode to the front of the field. The spectators cheered him on and his friends cheered him on.

When he crossed the finish line, Pino knew he had won. He was overjoyed and felt like he had realized his dream.

But then he noticed that one of his competitors had an accident and needed help. Pino didn't hesitate and stopped to help him. He helped him get up and took him to the finish line.

Although this caused him to lose his lead, Pino was proud of himself for helping his competitor. He had learned that racing wasn't everything in life and that it was also important to be there for others.

The moral of this story is that it is important to pursue your dreams and work hard to achieve your goals. But it's just as important to be there for others and help when they need help. Pino had learned that there was more to life than winning. It was about being there for each other and helping each other.

A JOURNEY INTO THE past

Pino and his dino friends were excited. They were to take part in a special expedition that would take them on a journey into the past. A scientist had built a time machine and invited the dinos to accompany him.

The dinos got into the time machine and the scientist explained that they would be traveling to the time of the dinosaurs, when the world looked different and the dinos ruled the land. The time machine started moving and the dinos were excited to see what they would experience.

When they arrived, they were overwhelmed by the beauty of nature. They saw rivers, forests and mountains that they had never seen before. But when they turned around, they saw something that shocked them. A giant T-Rex was coming toward them, roaring loudly. The dinos panicked and ran away.

When they got to safety, they saw that the T-Rex had not chased them. They decided to continue their journey and met many different dinosaurs. They saw a Diplodocus carrying them on its back through the forest and a Triceratops leading them to a water source.

But suddenly they heard a loud roar. They followed the sound and discovered that a dinosaur was in trouble. It was a small stegosaurus that was stuck in a swamp and couldn't get out on its own. The dinos decided to help him and worked together to free him.

When the Stegosaurus was finally free, he thanked his rescuers and said he was glad there were still good dinos around. The dinos were touched and realized that friendship and togetherness were more important than any adventure trip or discovery.

They finally returned to the time machine and said goodbye to the scientist. Pino and his friends were grateful for the experience they had had and vowed never to forget their friendship and togetherness.

PINO AND THE PREHISTORIC Safari

Pino and his friends had been on many adventures, but today they were in for something very special. They were going to go on a prehistoric safari and observe the dinosaurs in their natural environment. Pino couldn't wait to get out in the open and see the animals up close.

The friends met early in the morning and headed out into the jungle. It wasn't long before they spotted the first dinosaur. It was a triceratops, leisurely strolling by and eating some plants.

Pino and his friends watched the Triceratops for a while before they went on. They passed by a river where they saw some stegosaurs bathing. The friends decided to take a break and watch the stegosaurs splashing in the water.

As they continued walking, they heard a loud roar. It was a tyrannosaurus rex! The friends ran as fast as they could to get to safety. But when they reached a safe place, they realized that the T-Rex was not following them.

Pino and his friends were relieved and decided to continue their safari. They passed a large field full of brachiosaurs. These giant dinosaurs were so big that the friends felt like tiny ants.

The safari was an incredible experience for Pino and his friends. They had seen many dinosaurs and had learned a lot. Pino was impressed by the beauty and power of the animals.

On the way home, Pino thought about how important it is to respect and protect nature and its creatures. He knew he would share his experience with his friends and teach them why it is so important to take care of our environment.

Moral: It is important to protect and respect our environment and its inhabitants. We should strive to preserve the beauty and diversity of nature for future generations to enjoy.

An unexpected guest

Pino and his friends were in their hiding place when suddenly they heard a noise. It sounded like someone or something was nearby. They decided to move quietly to find out what was going on.

As they crept around the corner, they saw a small dinosaur. He was very shy and trembling with fear. Pino and his friends realized he was scared and decided to help him.

"What's wrong?" asked Pino to the little dinosaur. "Why are you so scared?"

"I'm alone," the little dinosaur answered. "I lost my family and I don't know how to find them."

Pino and his friends felt they had to help. They knew how it felt to be lost and have no family.

"Don't give up," Pino said. "We will help you find your family."

They began walking together through the jungle, looking for clues. It was difficult, but they didn't give up. They found footprints and followed them.

Finally they came to a big rock where they found a group of dinosaurs. The little dinosaur recognized his family and ran to them.

The family was so happy to find their lost son. They thanked Pino and his friends for their help and invited them to a feast.

Pino and his friends were very happy that they could help. They knew they had done a good deed and felt proud of it.

Moral: When we help others, we feel good and can have a positive impact on their lives. Even if we are sometimes scared or lost, there is always someone who can help us.

PINO MEETS THE T-REX

Pino and his friends are excited when they hear that the T-Rex has been spotted near Dino Land. They have heard a lot about the mighty T-Rex and are eager to meet him.

The friends head to the place where the T-Rex was last seen. On the way, Pino tells his friends that the T-Rex was a predator and hunted other dinosaurs to survive. But despite its size and strength, it also had enemies and was not invincible.

When they reach the place, they see the T-Rex in the distance and are impressed by its size and power. But suddenly they start to notice that he doesn't look happy and gives a sad growl.

Pino, who has always been a friendly and helpful dino, decides to help the T-Rex. He approaches him carefully and asks him what is wrong. The T-Rex tells him that he has been ostracized by the other dinosaurs and no one wants to talk to him.

Pino understands what it is like to be excluded and decides to help the T-Rex. He talks to his friends and convinces them to give the T-Rex a chance and talk to him.

After some time, the other dinosaurs slowly come closer and talk to the T-Rex. They realize that he is not as scary as they thought and that he is looking for friends and acceptance just like they are.

The friends decide to invite the T-Rex to live with them in Dino Land and play together. Pino is proud that he was able to help the T-Rex and that they all learned that you shouldn't judge anyone based on their looks or size.

Moral: You shouldn't rush to judgment or exclude others just because they look or act different. Everyone deserves a chance, and sometimes we can have surprises when we open up and get to know others.

THE SECRET OF THE CRYSTAL

Pino and his friends had had an exciting day in Dino World. They had crossed a river and explored a volcano. They were all tired now and were looking forward to taking a break. Suddenly a shiny crystal caught Pino's eye, sparkling in the sun. It was so beautiful and seemed magical.

"I'll take it with me," Pino said excitedly. But his friends cautioned him that it might be dangerous to touch the crystal or take it with him. But Pino was too curious and did it anyway.

The next day, Pino felt that the crystal was following him. He felt watched and uncomfortable. He decided to bring the crystal back, but when he arrived at the place where he found it, it had disappeared.

Pino was worried and afraid that something bad might happen. He began to investigate to find out what had happened to the crystal. He asked his friends and searched the neighborhood. Finally, he found out that the crystal actually had magical powers and that it had been stolen by an evil T-Rex.

Pino decided to get the crystal back and save his friends. He planned a ruse to outsmart the T-Rex and get the crystal back. With courage and skill, Pino and his friends managed to get the crystal back and defeat the T-Rex.

At the end of the day, Pino realized that it was wrong to just take the crystal without knowing what he was doing. He learned that you should be careful and get good information before you do anything. He also realized that it is important to stick together and stand up for each other in order to overcome difficult situations together.

Moral: It is important to be cautious and get well informed before doing anything. Cohesion and mutual support are key to overcoming difficult situations.

PINO AND THE DANGEROUS swamp

Pino and his friends, the Triceratops and the Stegosaurus, were searching for a lost crystal that was supposed to be hidden in the dangerous swamp. The swamp was known for its dangerous crocodiles and poisonous plants, but the three friends were determined to find the crystal.

When they reached the swamp, it was already dark, but they decided to go on anyway. Suddenly they heard a loud crack and a crocodile emerged from the water. Pino and his friends ran for their lives and hid in a nearby bush.

After they calmed down, they decided to make a plan. The Triceratops suggested that they run up the trees to escape the crocodiles. Stegosaurus had a different idea. He suggested that they swim across the swamp to escape the crocodiles.

Pino was skeptical, but he was also curious and decided to try the Stegosaurus' plan. They started swimming through the swamp, but they had to be careful not to get into the poisonous plants.

Suddenly, they noticed that they were not alone. A little baby dinosaur was trapped in the swamp. It had gotten tangled in the plants and couldn't get free. Pino and his friends decided to help the baby.

With their combined efforts, they managed to free the baby and rescue it from the swamp. They decided to take the baby back to his family, but they did not know where to find the family.

They began to explore the swamp and finally found the baby's family. The family was so grateful that they showed the three friends the way to the lost crystal.

When they found the crystal, Pino and his friends were overjoyed. Not only had they found the crystal, but they had also saved a little baby dinosaur. They learned that sometimes the most dangerous adventures are the best ones because you can help not only yourself, but others as well.

At the end of the day, Pino and his friends were tired but happy and proud of what they had accomplished. They decided that in the future they would always be ready to help others when they were in need.

A BRAVE RESCUE OPERATION

Pino and his dinosaur friends are on a walk through the jungle when they suddenly hear a loud rumbling sound. They run towards the sound and discover that a little Triceratops is trapped in a pit. The little dinosaur is scared and can't climb out on his own.

"We have to help him!" says Pino and his friends nod in agreement. But the pit is too deep for the dinos to just jump in. They have to find another plan. After some deliberation, Pino comes up with an idea: they could build a kind of ladder and rescue little Triceratops from the pit that way.

So the dinos set about gathering branches and leaves to build a ladder. They work together quickly and skillfully and soon the ladder is finished. Pino climbs down into the pit and calms the frightened Triceratops. Then he helps him climb up the ladder while his friends help from above.

Finally, little Triceratops is saved and his parents, who were nearby, come running to thank Pino and his friends. The dinos are proud of themselves and Pino tells them, "If we work together and help each other, we can do anything. Even if it gets hard, we must never give up."

The dinos are happy and head back to Dino Land. They know that they are a great team and that they will always be there for each other to help and have adventures.

THE TREASURE HUNTS

Pino and his dino friends were once again on the lookout for adventure. This time they had decided to look for a hidden treasure. They had heard about an old dinosaur that had buried a treasure a long time ago, but no one knew where it was hidden.

The dinosaur friends decided to work together to find the treasure. They searched the land and the forest, but they couldn't find anything. Finally, Pino had an idea. He had heard that there was an ancient temple nearby dedicated to the Lost treasure. Maybe they could find something there.

The group set out for the temple. They had to wade through a deep river and climb a steep mountain to get there. When they finally arrived, they were impressed by the size of the temple. The walls were covered with pictures of dinosaurs protecting the treasure.

The friends entered the temple and began searching for clues. They searched every corner of the temple and finally discovered a secret door. Behind it was a room where the treasure was hidden.

But as they approached the treasure, they realized they were not alone. A group of thieves had also set out to find the treasure. They were willing to do anything to get it.

The dino friends had to act quickly. They came up with a plan and decided to fool the thieves. They led them on a false trail and were finally able to get the treasure to safety.

Once they got the treasure to safety, the friends realized that the most important thing was not the treasure itself, but the friendship and cooperation they had shown to find and protect it. They realized that together is always better than alone and that they can accomplish anything if they stick together.

And so the dinosaur friends returned with a treasure much more valuable than gold: a deep bond and a valuable lesson about cooperation and friendship.

PINO AND THE HIDDEN cave

Pino and his dinosaur friends, Trixi the triceratops and Polly the pteranodon, had just finished playing a game of hide-and-seek when they suddenly heard a soft whisper. "What was that?" asked Pino, confused. Trixi and Polly listened intently. Then they heard it again, the whisper coming from a nearby rock formation.

"Let's go see!" said Pino determinedly and ran off, followed by Trixi and Polly. When they arrived at the rock wall, they discovered a small cave they had never noticed before. Pino didn't hesitate for long and crawled into the cave, followed by his friends.

Inside it was dark and narrow, but the dino friends managed to squeeze through the narrow cave. When they finally reached the end, they could hardly believe their eyes: in front of them was a huge pile of sparkling crystals.

"Wow, this is incredible!" exclaimed Polly excitedly. "I've never seen anything like it!" Trixi agreed with her and began to look more closely at the glittering stones. But Pino was skeptical. "I have a feeling something's not right here," he said quietly. "We'd better be careful."

Suddenly, a loud rumbling sounded, causing the ground beneath their feet to shake. "Oh no, it's an earthquake!" cried Trixi, startled. But Pino had another guess: "I think it's the T-Rex! He wants to take the treasure away from us!"

Immediately, the dino friends began to look for the way back to the cave entrance. But before they could reach it, the T-Rex appeared. "Give me the crystal treasure or I will eat you!" he roared menacingly.

But Pino did not give up. "We must not be intimidated!" he shouted to his friends. "Let's stick together and defend the treasure!" Together they faced the T-Rex and fought bravely for the crystal treasure.

In the end, they managed to put the T-Rex to flight and defend the treasure. "That was close!" sighed Trixi with relief. But Pino knew they always had to stick together and stand up for each other. "We are a strong community," he said proudly to his friends. "And if we stick together, we can handle any adventure!"

THE DINO ADVENTURE Camp

It was summer and Pino had signed up for a very special adventure. He would be attending a dino adventure camp! Together with other children, he would spend a week camping in the forest, exploring dinos and having exciting adventures.

On the first day, all the participants were welcomed by the camp leaders and divided into groups. Pino joined the group called "Triceratops." Together with the other children, he learned how to set up tents, make fire and cook food. Then the real adventure began: the search for the dinosaur tracks.

The group hiked through the forest looking for clues to dino fossils. Pino suddenly spotted a footprint much larger than any of the others. "That must have been a T-Rex!" he exclaimed excitedly. The other children were excited and the group decided to follow the track.

They finally came to a river that looked deep and dangerous. But the group had an idea: they built a raft out of branches and leaves and ventured down the river. It was an exciting adventure, but eventually they arrived safely on the other side.

There they found a cave that looked unimpressive from the outside. But when they went inside, they discovered an amazing dinosaur fossil collection. They marveled at the huge bones and teeth hidden in the cave.

But then they heard a loud roar from outside. It was a T-Rex that had followed them! The children panicked and didn't know what to do. But Pino had an idea: he remembered the fossils and decided to distract the T-Rex with a bone.

Fortunately, it worked and the T-Rex disappeared back into the forest. The group returned safely to camp and everyone was impressed with Pino's courage and resourcefulness.

At the end of the adventure, Pino received a special award for his bravery and use of his knowledge. He realized that sometimes you have to be brave and look at things differently to overcome difficult situations.

PINO AND THE CAMPFIRE

Pino had been looking forward to the Dino Adventure Camp for a long time. Finally, he could share his knowledge about dinosaurs with other children and experience adventures in nature. But when the time came, he suddenly felt insecure. What if he didn't make any friends or got lost in the wilderness?

As Pino sat around the campfire that first evening, he still felt unsafe. But then the other children began to talk. About their favorite dinosaurs, about the adventures they had already had, and about their hopes for the camp. Pino listened with fascination and quickly realized that he wasn't the only one who felt unsure.

The camp counselor had livened up the campfire with a few games, so the kids quickly got to talking. Pino had a lot of fun and felt more and more comfortable. But when it was time to go to sleep and the kids retreated to their tents, Pino felt the insecurity rising inside him again.

He lay awake for a long time thinking about what he could do to overcome his insecurity. Suddenly he remembered that he had given himself a special mission at camp: he really wanted to find a fossil. Digging up a dinosaur skeleton, that would be something special!

Pino got up and grabbed his flashlight. He decided to go searching again. It was pitch dark outside and Pino hesitated for a moment. But then he remembered what he had learned about the dinosaurs: they lived in a time when there were no streetlights and the night was much darker than it is now.

Pino trudged off, his flashlight firmly in hand. He wandered through the woods and the hills of the camp, looking for clues. Suddenly, he heard a noise. It was a cracking and crackling sound, as if something was moving through the foliage. Pino froze. What could that be?

But then he heard the crackling again and this time he noticed that it was coming from a certain direction. Cautiously, he continued walking and finally he discovered that the sound was caused by a small dinosaur searching for food in the dark. Pino could hardly believe his luck. He had actually seen a dinosaur in the wild!

When he came back to camp the next morning, he was full of energy and excitement. He told the other kids about his nighttime adventure and having them listen to him excited him even more. Suddenly, Pino knew he was on the right path. He would have many more adventures and find many more fossils.

A NIGHT IN THE OPEN

It was a beautiful day at Dino Adventure Camp and all the children had been watching the dinosaurs and playing games all day. Pino had made especially good friends with his new friends and they planned an outdoor adventure for that night.

They set up tents together and gathered wood for the campfire. After everything was ready, they sat around the campfire and shared their stories and adventures. Pino was so excited that he forgot it would soon be dark.

When it finally got dark, they suddenly heard a strange noise coming from the nearby forest. It sounded like a loud growl and the children suddenly felt uneasy.

Pino, the bravest of the group, decided they needed to find out what was making the noise. They pulled out their flashlights and followed the noise into the forest.

The farther they went, the louder the growl got and they realized it was coming from a small dinosaur that was caught in a trap. Pino and his friends saw that the dinosaur was scared and helpless.

They knew they had to help and decided to open the trap. It was hard, but finally they managed to free the dinosaur.

The little dinosaur was so happy and grateful that he wagged his tail at them. Pino and his friends took him back to their camp and spent the night taking care of him and finding him a new home.

The next morning, they finally found his family and left him in their care. Pino and his friends were proud to have helped the little dinosaur and learned that it is important to help others in need, even when it is difficult.

When they returned to camp, they were enthusiastically welcomed by their teachers and other children, who proudly told their story. Pino and his friends had experienced an unforgettable night and knew that they had made friends for life.

THE DINO DUEL

Pino was excited as he set off for the Dino Duel. It was the biggest event of the year in the prehistoric world. The best dino fighters would be competing against each other and Pino really wanted to be there to see his favorite dinos in battle.

When he arrived, the stadium was already full of people and dinos. The spectators were screaming and cheering as the fighters entered the ring. Pino watched in anticipation as the dinos attacked each other and tried to defeat the other.

Pino had a clear favorite to win the dino duel: T-Rex! But his best friend, Leo, was for Stegosaurus. The two boys were arguing about the winner of the duel when suddenly a noise silenced the crowd. A mighty dinosaur entered the ring: the Gigantosaurus!

Pino and Leo were equally excited about this giant dinosaur, which easily defeated its opponents. Pino thought that the Gigantosaurus was the strongest dino in the ring, but Leo was skeptical and thought that the T-Rex would beat him.

But then something unexpected happened: the Gigantosaurus got injured and had to leave the ring. The organizer of the dino duel turned to the spectators and asked if there was someone who would take the place of Gigantosaurus.

Pino and Leo looked at each other and nodded. "We can do this!" shouted Pino, pulling Leo into the ring. They would work together as a team and defeat the T-Rex.

The fight began and Pino and Leo bravely fought the T-Rex. They worked together to exploit its weaknesses and eventually they defeated it. The crowd cheered and Pino and Leo were the heroes of the dino duel.

At the end of the day, Pino realized that the dino duel was not only an exciting event, but also a lesson in cooperation and friendship. Together they could accomplish anything, even against a powerful opponent like the T-Rex.

PINO AGAINST THE TRICERATOPS

It was a sunny day in Dino Land when Pino and his friends set out to explore a new area. They walked through a dense forest and crossed a raging river until they finally reached an open plain.

Suddenly, they heard a loud roar coming from a distance. Pino and his friends followed the sound and discovered a big Triceratops moving towards them. The dinosaur was an impressive size with its large horns and thick skin.

Pino and his friends retreated, but the Triceratops stubbornly followed them. Suddenly they were on a cliff and could not run any further. The Triceratops was close on their heels and they had no choice but to confront him.

Pino stepped forward and bravely faced the Triceratops. He was ready for the duel and challenged the Triceratops. The Triceratops accepted the challenge and the duel began.

Pino and the Triceratops fought with all their strength, but neither could overpower the other. It seemed to be a draw, but Pino realized that the Triceratops was actually just afraid. He had only defended himself because he felt threatened.

Pino decided it was time to end the duel and find a peaceful solution. He took a step back and signaled to the Triceratops that he was not a threat. The Triceratops calmed down and retreated.

Pino and his friends returned home and told everyone about their adventure. They had learned that sometimes you just have to find a peaceful solution to resolve conflicts. It was an important moment for Pino and his friends because they had learned that courage and peace can go hand in hand.

THE ATTACK OF THE CARNIVORES

Pino and his friends were on a dino trip and had so much fun! They wandered through the forest, exploring fossils and watching peaceful herbivores like Brachiosaurus. But as they were heading home, they suddenly heard strange noises coming from the bushes.

Pino and his friends were curious and decided to get to the bottom of it. They got closer and discovered to their horror that a group of carnivores was watching them! A Velociraptor, an Allosaurus, and a Tyrannosaurus Rex were nearby and hungry.

Pino and his friends tried to escape, but the carnivores were too fast. Suddenly, an idea came to Pino. He remembered that the herbivores often stood together in groups to defend themselves. Pino called his friends together and they formed a group to show the carnivores that they were not alone.

The carnivores were surprised and hesitated for a moment. Pino took this chance and ordered his friends to shout loudly and shake branches to intimidate the carnivores. The strategy worked and the carnivores retreated.

Pino and his friends were relieved, but also grateful for the cooperation and support they received from each other. They had learned that it was important to stick together in difficult situations and not give up.

When they returned to Dino Camp, they proudly told of their adventure and how they had put the carnivores to flight. The other children marveled at their bravery and felt more secure knowing that Pino and his friends would always stand up for each other.

The moral of the story is that cooperation and cohesion are very important in difficult situations. Even though it can be difficult at times, we should always try to be there for each other and support each other.

AN ESCAPE THROUGH THE jungle

Pino and his friends, Velociraptor and Stegosaurus, were out in the jungle looking for new adventures. They had just discovered a new cave and decided to explore it more closely. But suddenly they heard a menacing growl and realized that they were not alone.

A pack of hungry carnivores was on the prowl and had already spotted Pino and his friends. They quickly realized that they were in great danger and decided to flee. But the jungle was impenetrable and the pack quickly caught up.

Pino and his friends ran for their lives, hoping for a chance to escape the carnivores. They jumped over rivers, climbed over rocks, and ran through the dense brush. But the carnivores did not let up and were always close on their heels.

Suddenly, Pino spotted a cave and called out to his friends to run into it. The cave was narrow and dark, but it was the only way to escape the carnivores. Pino and his friends hid and held their breath.

The pack arrived at the cave and sniffed around to find their prey. However, Pino had an idea. He took some rocks and threw them in a different direction to distract the carnivores. The tactic worked and the carnivores followed the sound.

Pino and his friends took the chance and ran out of the cave. They ran as fast as they could to avoid being caught up by the carnivores again. After a while they reached a river and Pino had another idea. They built a raft out of branches and leaves and set across the river.

The carnivores had given up the chase and Pino and his friends were finally safe. They breathed a sigh of relief and headed back to their cave. On the way, they talked about how they could protect themselves from the carnivores in the future and concluded that they should always be on guard.

The adventure had taught Pino and his friends that one should always have a plan when in danger. It was important to make decisions quickly and to act courageously. They had also learned that in difficult situations you should always stick together and be there for each other.

PINO AS AN EXPLORER

Pino was a curious and adventurous dinosaur who was always looking for new discoveries. One day he decided to try his hand as an explorer and set off on an expedition into the unexplored jungle.

Accompanied by his friends, Triceratops and Stegosaurus, Pino set off into the deep and dense forest. They crossed rivers and crossed mountains, always looking for new tracks and signs of life.

But as they ventured deep into the jungle, they suddenly heard a loud growl. Pino immediately realized that it must be coming from a dangerous predator and warned his friends. Together they sought shelter and tried to escape the growl.

Suddenly they discovered an old abandoned hut and decided to hide there. Pino, the intrepid dino, decided to go exploring on his own. He searched the hut and found a map that led him to a hidden temple.

Pino and his friends decided to follow the path of the map. They crossed a raging river and fought their way through thick bushes. Finally, they reached the temple and were amazed at what they saw.

In the middle of the temple, they found a huge crystal that sparkled like a rainbow. Pino immediately realized that it was the largest crystal he had ever seen. He also knew that the crystal had enormous power and was invaluable.

Suddenly they heard the growling again and realized they were surrounded by the carnivores. Pino knew they had no time to lose and called his friends together. Together they decided to protect the crystal and drive away the predators.

They fought bravely against the carnivores and finally managed to defeat them. Pino and his friends returned from the jungle triumphant, proud that they had succeeded as explorers and protected the precious crystal.

But Pino also realized that power is not everything in life and that it is more important to value friendship and cohesion. Thus ended the adventure of the brave dinosaur who ventured deep into the jungle as an explorer and learned an important lesson about life.

THE DISCOVERY OF THE pterosaur

It was a sunny day at Dino Adventure Camp, and Pino was excited when he learned that they were going on a field trip into the mountains today. They were going to look for fossils and maybe even discover a new dinosaur!

Pino packed his bag with everything he needed: binoculars, a hammer, a magnifying glass, and a book about dinosaurs. He was ready for adventure!

The group was hiking through the mountains when suddenly Pino saw something flashing on a Rock. He ran forward to examine it and found a small, iridescent piece of Rock. He took it in his hand and noticed that it looked different from all the rocks he had seen before.

Pino was so excited about his discovery that he told the rest of the group about it. The leader of the expedition examined the stone and said, "Pino, I think you just found something very special!"

They headed back to camp to examine the stone more closely. They hooked it up to a microscope and could see that it contained tiny bone fragments. It was a fossil!

Pino was so excited that he spent the rest of the day researching books to find out what animal it might have been. Finally, he came across a picture of a pterosaur that looked like the fossil!

Pino was thrilled. He had indeed discovered a new fossil, and it was a pterosaur! He couldn't wait to share his discovery with the world.

The adventure had taught Pino that with curiosity and determination, you can accomplish incredible things. He was proud that he had made his discovery and hoped that he would have many more adventures.

A DAY AT THE BEACH

It was a beautiful day and Pino and his friends had decided to take a trip to the beach. They packed their bathing suits and a picnic bag full of goodies and set off.

When they arrived at the beach, they were thrilled to see the soft sand and the blue sea. They ran to the water and jumped in, swimming and splashing around.

Suddenly they heard a loud crashing sound and saw a big wave coming towards them. They tried to get out of the water as fast as they could, but the wave was too fast and caught them all.

When they resurfaced, they saw that their picnic bag and bathing suit were gone. They were disappointed and sad. But then they saw something that caught their attention.

It was a group of sea creatures sitting on a rock and looking sad. Pino and his friends went closer and saw that a big shark was threatening the sea animals.

They knew they had to act and decided to help the sea animals. They gathered wood and built a fire to scare off the shark. Then they started digging holes in the sand with their hands to create a barrier between the shark and the sea animals.

The shark was scared off by the fire and the barrier and swam away. Pino and his friends had saved the sea animals and felt very proud.

They decided to spend the rest of the day on the beach and forget about the picnic. They played and built sand castles, and when the sun went down, they sat on the beach and watched the waves come ashore.

They knew they had a memorable day at the beach and that they could be there for each other in difficult situations. Pino and his friends realized that it was important to help others and that if they worked together, they could accomplish anything.

PINO AND THE SEA CREATURES

It was a sunny day at the beach and Pino was very excited. Today he would explore the sea and meet all the wonderful sea creatures he had heard so much about. Together with his friends, he went to the shore and put on his water wings. They dove into the clear blue water and began their exploration.

As they swam a little further, they suddenly saw a large shadow below them. Pino was excited and eager to see what they were about to see. It was a huge turtle swimming calmly and majestically through the water. The children were excited and tried to get as close as they could to pet it.

Suddenly they saw something else in the water. It was a small fish caught in a plastic bag. The children saw that he was begging for help and they decided to help him. They cut open the bag and the fish were able to escape. The children realized that the garbage that people throw into the sea is not only bad for the environment, but also for the animals.

As they continued swimming, they saw many different fish and even a crab. They watched as the fish swam in schools and as the crab moved across the sand. Pino was fascinated by all the different colors and shapes.

Suddenly they heard a noise behind them and turned around. It was a dolphin jumping out of the water and diving back into the water. The children were excited and shouted with joy. The dolphin swam alongside them and showed them his tricks.

Pino and his friends had so much fun that they didn't even notice how quickly the time passed. When they swam back to the beach, they were sad that their adventure in the sea was over. But they were also grateful for all the wonderful sea creatures they had met.

On the beach, they saw many people throwing their trash on the ground instead of putting it in the trash cans. Pino and his friends were shocked and decided to ask their parents and teachers to start a campaign to clean the beaches and the seas.

Pino and his friends learned a lot that day about the wonders of the sea, but also about the importance of protecting our planet and its inhabitants.

A DIVE IN THE OCEAN

Pino and his friends Max and Emma were very excited when they finally arrived at the ocean. They had been looking forward to this day for a long time, because they really wanted to go diving and discover the beauty of the ocean.

The three friends put on their diving suits and put on their diving masks. Then they jumped into the water and dove down into the depths of the sea. It was breathtaking! All around them swam colorful fish, starfish, and coral.

Suddenly they heard a loud crash. Max pointed to a big rock and they saw that a group of sharks had gathered there. The three friends were very frightened because they knew that sharks can be dangerous.

Pino suggested that they dive away slowly and quietly so that the sharks would not be disturbed. But suddenly Max was attacked by a shark! Pino and Emma were horrified and knew they had to act quickly.

Pino remembered a story his father had told him when he was little. In the story, a diver had fought off a shark with a harpoon-type weapon.

Pino quickly swam back to the surface and retrieved such a weapon from their boat.

As Pino swam back to Max and Emma to fight off the shark, he noticed that the shark had only bitten by accident because it was disturbed by a fisherman's hook that was still in its mouth. Pino removed the hook and the shark quickly swam away.

The three friends were relieved and continued diving when they suddenly saw a group of dolphins. The dolphins swam around them and showed them their best tricks. Pino, Max and Emma were thrilled and thankful that they could experience this wonderful moment.

At the end of the day, the three friends were tired but happy. They knew that they had learned a valuable lesson: That you cannot foresee all the dangers of the ocean, but that you can act with calm and prudence in difficult situations. And that one should always respect and protect the beauty of the sea.

THE ENCOUNTER WITH the megalodon

Pino and his friends set out for the ocean. They wanted to go on a dive and discover the sea creatures. When they arrived at the beach, they quickly put on their diving gear and jumped into the water.

Underwater, they saw beautiful coral reefs and colorful fish. But suddenly they heard a loud noise. It sounded like a huge scream. Pino turned around and saw a huge shadow in the water.

It was a megalodon! This prehistoric shark was almost as big as a school bus and had huge sharp teeth. Pino and his friends were scared when they saw the huge shark. But they knew they had to stay calm.

The megalodon was getting closer and Pino had an idea. He got out his camera and started taking pictures of the megalodon. The megalodon swam around them and Pino was able to take some amazing photos. After a while, the megalodon swam away again.

Pino and his friends swam back to the beach. They were relieved that they were safe and that they had seen this incredible creature. Pino had also learned something important. He knew that it was important to respect and admire animals in their natural environment.

When they returned to the beach, they talked to other tourists who had also heard about the megalodon. They told them about their adventure and showed them the photos they had taken. The others were thrilled and asked how they had the courage to be so close to this huge shark.

Pino and his friends just smiled. They knew it wasn't about courage, but respect and admiration for the beauty and wonder of nature.

Pino and the ghost dinos

Pino and his friends had already had many adventures in the prehistoric world. But this time they had come across something they had never seen before. It was a collection of strange dinosaur skeletons that glowed in the dark.

The kids were fascinated by the glowing bones and decided to find out what it was all about. They followed the tracks that led them to a dark forest. As they went deeper into the forest, it became more and more eerie.

Suddenly they heard strange noises and felt the ground shake beneath their feet. Then a huge dinosaur appeared in front of them, glowing and sparkling. It looked like a T-Rex, but it was much bigger than any T-Rex they had ever seen before.

The children were scared at first, but Pino quickly realized that the dino was harmless. He also seemed interested in the children and invited them to follow him. They eventually came to a cave guarded by glowing dinosaur skeletons.

In the cave they met an old, wise dinosaur who explained to them that these bones came from dinos that had lived many years ago and had been infected by a mysterious virus. The virus had made them glow and destroyed their bodies, but their bones remained.

The old dinosaur also told the children about a legend about a cursed treasure that was supposed to be hidden in the cave. The children were excited about the idea of finding the treasure and started searching for clues.

They fought various traps and puzzles they encountered along the way, and eventually they found the treasure. It was a golden egg that could heal all the dinos in the world.

When they took the egg, they were attacked by a group of ghost dinos. They were the skeletons of the dinos that had been destroyed by the virus. But Pino and his friends fought bravely against the ghost dinos and managed to escape.

When they returned the treasure to their friend, the old dino, all the dinos in the world were cured. The children realized that sometimes it takes courage to accomplish something important, and that cooperation and friendship can help overcome any challenge.

A SPOOKY NIGHT FORESTS

Pino and his friends made their way into the forest. It was already dark and the fog hung low among the trees. The leaves rustled in the wind and the animals had fallen silent. It was spooky, but Pino was brave and wanted to prove to his friends that he wasn't afraid.

They followed a narrow path that wound through the forest. The trees were so dense that hardly any light came through and it got darker and darker the further they went. Pino felt his heart beat faster and he felt more and more uncomfortable. But he didn't want to admit that he was afraid, so he kept walking.

Suddenly they heard a strange noise. It was a creaking, as if someone was walking on an old wooden floor. The children froze. Pino wanted to go ahead to see what it was, but his friends pulled him back.

But then, out of the darkness, a figure emerged. It was an old woman with a gnarled walking stick. She had white hair and wore a dirty apron. Pino was surprised when she walked past them without paying attention to them.

The children followed the woman and noticed that she was going into a small house. The house looked old and abandoned, but the light seemed to still be on. Pino and his friends cautiously approached the house and looked through the window.

Inside there was the old woman sitting and reading a book. She was no longer creepy, but looked friendly. Pino thought that maybe she knew something about the forest and decided to approach her.

They knocked on the door and when they were invited in, Pino asked the woman about the forest and if she knew why it was so creepy. The woman replied that the forest was not scary, but that it was the stories and rumors that people told.

The children learned that it is important to distinguish truth from rumors and not to be influenced by prejudices and fears. Pino and his friends said goodbye to the kind old woman and left the house. As they left the forest, Pino looked back and said to his friends, "The forest isn't as scary as we thought, we just have to be brave."

And so the children learned that in life there is often more appearance than reality and that it is important to be brave and not to be intimidated by rumors and prejudices.

THE HAUNTED HOUSE

Pino and his friends, Lily and Tom, were looking for adventure. One day they heard about an old abandoned house on the outskirts of town that was supposedly haunted by ghosts. The children decided to explore the haunted house and find out if it was really inhabited by ghosts.

They set out in the evening and arrived at the old house, which looked even spookier in the dark. The children carefully crept through the tall grass and approached the house. Suddenly they heard an eerie creaking and cracking sound, as if the house had come alive. The children trembled with fear, but they decided to go on.

When they entered the house, they found everything dusty and untidy. The furniture was old and broken and there were cobwebs everywhere. Suddenly they heard a noise that sounded like a whisper. The children were startled and stopped. "It must be a ghost," whispered Lily.

Pino and Tom didn't dare go any further, but Lily was brave and desperate to know where the whispering came from. She followed the sound until she found a door that was half open. When she opened the door, she found a small room with an old book and a candle on a table.

The children decided to open the book and found a story inside about a missing treasure that was supposed to be hidden in the house. The children were excited and decided to find the treasure. They searched the whole house and finally found a box of gold coins and jewels.

Suddenly they heard a whisper again and this time they also saw a figure. It was a man who had lived in the house a long time ago. He told the children his story and was grateful that they had found the treasure. He also explained that he was not a ghost, but that he had only entered the house secretly to look for his hidden treasure.

The children were relieved and happy that they had found the treasure and that there was no ghost in the house. They returned home and divided the treasure fairly. Pino and his friends had not only had an exciting adventure, but they had also learned that you don't always have to be afraid and that you should always be brave to make your dreams come true.

PINO AND THE CASTLE of horror

Pino and his friends were on a trip to the mountains. They hiked all day until they saw an old castle in the distance. The castle looked so old and creepy that they couldn't pass up the chance to explore it.

When they reached the castle, they noticed that the door was open. They entered and found themselves in a large room full of cobwebs and dust. Suddenly they heard a strange noise and when they turned around, they were standing in front of a large gate.

Curious, they opened the gate and found a room full of treasures and gold coins. They were so excited that they were not aware that they had fallen into a trap. Suddenly, the gate closed behind them and they were trapped in the room.

The friends started looking for an exit when they encountered a figure that looked like a ghost. The ghost said that he was the original owner of the castle and that he demanded that the friends give him back his treasure.

Pino and his friends realized that they were in trouble and that they had no choice but to satisfy the ghost. They handed him his treasure and the ghost turned into a friendly figure.

The spirit told them that he had died from greed for wealth and power and that he never had a chance to change. He urged the friends to learn from his mistakes and never let greed get the better of them.

Pino and his friends learned a valuable lesson that day. They left the castle promising to always listen to their hearts and never give in to greed. They returned home and told everyone about their adventure in the Castle of Horror.

The moral of the story is that greed for wealth and power will never lead to anything good and that it is important to listen to your heart and never abandon your friends.

AN EERIE ENCOUNTER

Pino and his friends were on a camping trip in the mountains. They had spent the whole day hiking through the forest and exploring nature. But as the sun set and night fell, they realized they were lost.

Pino and his friends were suddenly alone and scared in the dark forest. They were afraid of wild animals and unknown sounds coming from the darkness. Suddenly they heard a terrible scream echoing through the forest. They looked around and saw something scary: a creature that looked like a creepy ghost was floating towards them.

Pino and his friends ran as fast as they could to escape the ghost. They knew they had to think of something quickly to survive. Finally, they found a small cave and crawled inside. It was dark and narrow, but at least they were safe from the ghost.

Once they felt safe in the cave, they began to think of a way to get out of the forest. Pino suggested that they could use the starry sky to find their way out of the forest. He explained that the North Star always points north and that they could use it to determine their direction.

Pino and his friends crawled out of the cave and looked up at the clear night sky. The North Star was bright and clearly visible. They followed it and after some time they reached a clearing in the forest. In the distance, they saw a village that could be reached from here.

They followed the path and finally reached the village. They were relieved and grateful that they had survived the night. They learned that sometimes there are difficult situations, but that there is always a solution if you stick together and think creatively.

The fight against the zombie dinosaurs

It was a sunny day at the dinosaur Park and Pino was exploring with his friends. Suddenly, they heard a loud growl that seemed to come from far away. As they got closer, they saw a group of dinosaurs coming toward them. But there was something strange about them. Their skin was rotten and they moved slowly and awkwardly. They were not normal dinosaurs, but zombie dinosaurs!

Pino and his friends panicked as the zombie dinosaurs got closer and closer. They ran away as fast as they could, but it seemed like the zombie dinosaurs were getting faster and faster. They ran into the forest, but even there they were not safe. The zombie dinosaurs followed them at every turn.

Suddenly, Pino remembered that he had an emergency plan that he had learned in school. He said to his friends, "We have to hide and wait for the zombie dinosaurs to pass." They ran to a nearby bush and hid in it. The zombie dinosaurs ran past them without noticing them.

When the zombie dinosaurs disappeared, Pino and his friends ran to the Dinosaur Park office for help. There they met the park ranger, who explained that the zombie dinosaurs had been infected by a virus that turned their bodies into undead creatures. The park ranger explained that they had to fight the zombie dinosaurs to save the dinosaur park.

Pino and his friends were ready to meet the challenge. The park ranger gave them weapons and explained that the only way they could defeat the zombie dinosaurs was by shooting them in the brain. Pino and his friends went back to the park and started the fight against the zombie dinosaurs.

It was a tough fight, but after many fights and many shots, Pino and his friends managed to defeat all the Zombiesaurs. They saved the dinosaur park and became heroes. The park ranger thanked them and said that they showed that with courage and determination you can overcome any challenge.

Pino and his friends learned that day that you should never give up and that you should always fight to do the right thing. They were proud to have saved the dinosaur park and they knew that they were always ready to face other challenges.

PINO AS AN APPRENTICE magician

Pino was a little dinosaur who had always been passionate about magic. He had read many books about magic tricks and spells and was eager to learn how to do magic.

One day, Pino heard that there was a powerful wizard nearby who was willing to take on an apprentice. Pino was excited and decided to set out to meet the wizard.

When he arrived, however, the wizard was very suspicious. He had many requests from young dinosaurs who wanted to learn magic, but none of them had been successful yet.

But Pino did not give up. He asked the wizard to give him a chance and promised to work hard and do everything he could to become a good apprentice wizard.

The wizard finally agreed and began to teach Pino the basics of magic. Pino learned quickly and was excited about the different magic tricks he could learn.

One day, the wizard challenged Pino to invent his own magic spell. Pino was excited, but also a little nervous. He didn't know if he would be able to invent a good spell.

Pino worked hard on it and after many hours, he had finally invented a spell that he called "The Dino Spell". He was very excited to impress the wizard and try out his new spell.

But when Pino performed his spell, something strange happened. The spell didn't work as expected and suddenly he turned into a frog!

Pino was horrified and the wizard was furious. He said that Pino was not good enough to be a sorcerer's apprentice and sent him away.

Pino was very sad and thought that he would never be a good wizard. But then he remembered that he had to realize his mistakes and work on them to become better. He decided to work hard and ask the wizard for forgiveness.

Pino returned to the wizard and asked for a second chance. This time he worked even harder and practiced the "Dino Spell" over and over until it worked perfectly.

The wizard was impressed with Pino's progress and realized that Pino was really a good apprentice magician. He accepted his apology and gave him a second chance.

Pino was happy and grateful for the opportunity to learn from such an experienced magician. He knew he still had a lot to learn, but he was willing to work hard and improve his skills.

The moral of this story is that you must always work hard and recognize your mistakes in order to succeed.

THE MAGIC OF DINOSAURS

Pino was a little dinosaur who lived in a world full of magic and adventure. One day he heard about a powerful spell that would allow him to use the powers of dinosaurs and accomplish incredible things.

Pino was excited by this idea and decided to become a sorcerer's apprentice. He asked his friend, the wise Stegosaurus, if he could help him become a wizard. Stegosaurus was a wise dinosaur and explained to Pino that wizards need a lot of practice and patience to master their skills.

Pino was willing to work hard and began to focus on his magic studies. He learned the basics of magic, how to cast spells, and how to gather energy from his surroundings. It wasn't easy, but Pino didn't give up and worked hard on his skills.

One day, when Pino was about to learn a new spell, he suddenly felt a strong energy around him. It was the energy of the dinosaurs that had accumulated in the air. Pino felt that he could use this energy to strengthen his magic powers.

He concentrated on his breathing and closed his eyes. When he opened them again, he could feel the magic of the dinosaurs around him. He felt himself getting stronger and more powerful and knew he was ready to try his new spell.

Pino took a deep breath and cast the spell he had learned. Immediately, the air around him turned into a sparkling display of color, and little dinosaurs in all the colors of the rainbow appeared around him.

Pino was excited about his new power and knew he would only use it for good. He had learned that magic can be a wonderful power when used responsibly. And so he decided to develop his abilities further to help other dinosaurs in need and create a world full of magic and adventure.

PINO AND THE MYSTERIOUS magic wand

Pino was a little dinosaur who dreamed of adventures. One day he heard about a mysterious magic wand that was supposed to be hidden somewhere in the jungle. The magic wand was said to give incredible powers to whoever found it.

Pino was immediately excited and decided to find the wand. He set off into the deep jungle, full of courage and determination. The path was difficult and dangerous, but Pino did not give up.

Finally, he reached a clearing and saw something that made his breath catch. In front of him stood a huge T-Rex, staring at him menacingly. Pino hesitated for a moment, but then he remembered his parents' stories about the bravery and courage needed in dangerous situations. Pino decided to be brave and face the T-Rex.

He pulled out his little dinosaur spear and ran toward the T-Rex. The fight was tough and Pino had a lot of trouble, but he didn't give up. With a lot of skill and a portion of luck, Pino was able to defeat the T-Rex.

Exhausted and tired, Pino continued on his way. Finally, he reached a small temple where the magic wand was supposed to be hidden. Pino entered the temple and found the wand in a corner. He carefully took it in his hand and immediately felt an energy flowing through his body. The wand gave him incredible powers and he felt invincible.

Pino proudly returned to his village and showed everyone his new wand. The other dinos were very impressed and asked him how he had found the wand. Pino explained that it was his courage and determination that had helped him find the wand.

The moral of the story is that you can accomplish anything if you just have the courage and determination to try. Even if it is difficult and dangerous, we should never give up and always be brave.

A JOURNEY BACK IN TIME to the Middle Ages

Pino and his friends were excited. Today they had learned about the Middle Ages in school and were excited about knights, kings and castles. Suddenly, Pino remembered that he had found an old book in the library that was about a wizard who had built a time machine. If they could find and repair this machine, they could travel to the Middle Ages themselves!

Together, Pino and his friends made their way to the library. There they found the old book and read the instructions. They assembled the time machine and got in. Pino pressed the button and suddenly they were surrounded by a bright light.

When they opened their eyes again, they were in a green meadow. Pino looked around and saw that they had indeed traveled to the Middle Ages. They saw a castle on the horizon and decided to go there.

On the way, they met a knight in shining armor. The knight asked them who they were and where they came from. Pino explained everything to him and the knight invited them to accompany him to the castle.

When they reached the castle, they were greeted by the king. He was delighted to receive a visit from such unusual guests. He invited them to a feast where they ate all kinds of delicacies and exchanged stories.

Suddenly they were attacked by a horde of robbers. The king and his knights fought bravely, but they were outnumbered. Pino and his friends decided to help. Using Pino's magic wand, they managed to confuse the robbers and give the knights an advantage in the fight.

When the robbers were defeated, the king thanked Pino and his friends for their help. They were declared guests of honor and stayed in the castle for a few more days. Eventually, however, they had to travel back to the present.

Pino and his friends returned to the present with many great stories and experiences. Not only did they have a great time in the Middle Ages, but they had also learned that it is always important to help others and stick together.

KNIGHT PINO AND THE Dragon Fight

Once upon a time there was a little boy named Pino who dreamed of being a brave knight and having fearless adventures. One day his dream came true when he was magically sent back in time and found himself in a world full of knights and castles.

Pino found himself in a great castle where he met an old knight who explained to him that the kingdom was threatened by a terrible dragon. The dragon had attacked the village near the castle and reduced everything to rubble. The king had therefore decided to organize a battle against the dragon to save his kingdom.

Pino was eager to help and joined the knights to defeat the dragon. He learned that the dragon lived in a cave in the mountains and that only a brave knight could defeat him.

So Pino set out for the cave, accompanied by some brave knights. When they reached the cave, the dragon was already waiting for them. He was huge and spewed fire from his mouth.

The knights fought the dragon, but they had difficulty harming him. Pino, not knowing what to do, remembered an old spell that the old knight had taught him in the castle. He pulled out his wand and called out the magic words.

Suddenly a ray of light appeared and hit the dragon, weakening it. The knights took this opportunity and attacked the dragon with their swords. Finally, Pino managed to land the final blow on the dragon and it fell to the ground dead.

The knights were relieved and thanked Pino for his help. The king was so happy that he knighted Pino and declared him the hero of the kingdom.

Pino realized that everyone was capable of being brave and that sometimes even a small magic wand can have a great effect. He learned that in life it is important to help others and that it is worth fighting for what you love and what you stand for.

And so Pino returned to the present, knowing that he was a true knight and hero, and he could hardly wait to continue his adventures.

A FEAST IN THE CASTLE courtyard

It was a beautiful day in the castle courtyard. The sun was shining and the birds were chirping happily. All around there were busy people making preparations for the upcoming feast. It was going to be a big party for all the inhabitants of the castle and everyone was excited.

Pino, the little dinosaur, was there too. He looked around and admired the many colorful pennants hanging among the trees in the castle courtyard. He could smell the delicious aroma of roasted meat and freshly baked bread coming from the kitchen.

Suddenly, Pino heard a familiar voice. It was the knight who had saved him when he was in trouble. The knight came to Pino and asked him if he would help him prepare for the feast.

Pino did not hesitate for a moment and said yes. Together with the knight, Pino helped set up the tables and align the chairs. They also placed many colorful flowers on the tables and decorated the castle courtyard with colorful banners.

When everything was ready, the party was opened. The residents of the castle came together and enjoyed the food and entertainment. There were knights waving their swords and musicians playing happy songs. Pino danced with the children and had a lot of fun.

But suddenly Pino noticed that someone was missing. It was the stable boy who always brought him the delicious grass. Pino asked around and finally learned that the stable boy was sick and in bed.

Pino decided to give the stable boy a little treat. He ran into the garden and looked for the most delicious carrots he could find. Then he went into the castle and sought out the kitchen. There he asked the cooks to bake him a carrot cake.

When everything was ready, Pino took the carrot cake to the stable boy. The stable boy was so happy about the surprise that he cried with joy.

Pino realized that life is not all about parties and fun. It's also about helping others and making them happy. Pino learned that small gestures can go a long way and that it is important to be attentive to the needs of others.

The party in the castle courtyard was an unforgettable experience for Pino. Not only did he have fun and enjoy himself, but he also learned how important it is to help others and make them happy.

THE RETURN TO DINO Land

It was a sunny day and Pino and his friends were in the park. While they were playing, they suddenly discovered an old, rusty key. Pino was curious and decided to examine it more closely. He noticed that the key fit exactly into the lock of an old book he had found some time ago. He put the key in the lock and turned it carefully.

Suddenly, a loud hiss sounded and a dusty cloud filled the room. When the dust settled, Pino and his friends were surrounded by green forests and giant dinosaurs! They were back in dino land!

Pino and his friends couldn't believe they were back in the world of dinosaurs. They decided to explore the surroundings and met friendly dinosaurs who greeted them warmly. Pino was especially excited when he met a friendly Stegosaurus who helped him cross a huge bridge.

But suddenly they heard a loud roar and realized that a large and ferocious T-Rex was blocking their path. Pino and his friends ran for their lives, but the T-Rex was too fast for them.

At that moment, Pino remembered the old book he had found. Maybe it could help them escape from this dicey situation. He opened the book and began to read. Suddenly, a magical wind swept through the air and enveloped the friends.

When the wind died down, they noticed that they were all holding wands. Pino realized that they were all powerful wizards now and decided to defeat the T-Rex with their magic.

Pino and his friends created a powerful spell that enveloped the T-Rex and turned it into a friendly dinosaur. The dino gave them a friendly greeting and Pino and his friends continued their adventures in Dino Land.

At the end of the day, when it was time to leave, Pino found the lock again and closed the old book with the key. They returned to the park and Pino and his friends knew that they would never forget what they had learned in this magical world of dinosaurs: that there is always a solution if you stick together and believe in each other.

PINO AND THE DISCOVERY of the flints

Pino and his friends were on a trip to the forest. They were playing hide and seek and collecting beautiful stones. Suddenly they discovered a cave they had never seen before. Curious, they ventured into the darkness and were amazed to see that the walls glittered and sparkled.

As they got closer, they saw that they were flints. Pino and his friends collected some of them and found out that when they hit each other, they sent sparks flying. They were delighted and played with the flints for hours.

When evening came, they started on their way home. But on their way back, they noticed that the forest was on fire. They were shocked and didn't know what to do. Then Pino remembered the flints and hit two of them on each other. Sparks immediately flew, igniting the dry leaves.

They used the flints to create a circle of fire around themselves and called for help. The fire department came and put out the fire. Pino and his friends were relieved and proud that they were able to contain the fire because of their discovery.

Pino realized that sometimes something that seems trivial to us at first glance can be very valuable in certain situations. He also learned that it is important to take responsibility and help others in need. His friends and he decided that every time they saw flints, they would remember how important they can be and always keep them carefully.

The next day, Pino told his father about the discovery and they decided to donate the flints to the local museum so that others could learn about them as well.

The discovery of the flints was an exciting adventure that taught Pino and his friends not only a lot of fun, but also an important lesson about responsibility and cooperation.

A new dino baby

It was a sunny day in Dino Land and Pino and his friends were out exploring. They were walking through the forest, past the tall trees and the little rivers. Suddenly they heard a loud noise coming from a bush. Cautiously, they crept closer and saw a little baby dinosaur helplessly alone.

Pino and his friends immediately realized that the little baby dinosaur had lost its family and decided to save it. They knew they couldn't leave it alone, so they took it with them and decided to help it find a new family.

They searched Dino Land for families who could adopt the little baby, but each time they were disappointed. It seemed that no family was willing to take the baby.

Pino and his friends were sad, but they decided not to give up on the baby. They decided to put it in a safe and warm place for the time being until they found a solution.

They spent the next few days feeding the baby and keeping him company. They told him about their adventures in Dino Land and played with him. The baby became happier and happier and began to grow.

One day, when they were exploring again, they met a group of dinosaurs who wanted to adopt the baby. Pino and his friends were happy and relieved that the baby had finally found a new family.

They said goodbye to the baby and watched as he became comfortable in the arms of his new family. Pino and his friends were proud that they had rescued the baby and helped him find a new family.

They realized that sometimes the greatest adventures are not the ones where you put yourself in danger, but the ones where you help others. They had learned that even the smallest of us can accomplish great things if we are willing to go out of our way to help others.

THE WORRIES OF THE Dino parents

It was a beautiful day in Dino Land and Pino and his friends were playing together as usual. They ran around, played tag, and ate delicious fruit. But suddenly they heard a loud crying. They ran in the direction of the sound and found two dinosaur parents who were very sad.

"What's wrong?" asked Pino worriedly.

"Our baby dinosaur has disappeared," sobbed the mommy dinosaur. "We've been looking everywhere for it, but it's not to be found."

Pino and his friends decided to help the dino parents find their baby. They split up and searched in different parts of Dino Land. For hours they searched for the missing baby dinosaur, but it was nowhere to be found.

Slowly it was getting dark and Pino and his friends were tired and hungry. They decided to return to the cave of the dino parents and tell them the sad news.

However, when they reached the cave, they saw the missing baby dinosaur sitting hidden in a bush. It seemed happy and unharmed.

"We found it!" exclaimed Pino delightedly, lifting the baby up. "It was hiding in the bushes."

The dino parents were overjoyed and thanked Pino and his friends for their help. They invited everyone to a feast to express their gratitude.

During the feast, the dino parents talked about their worries and fears as parents in Dino Land. They shared how hard it can sometimes be to protect and care for their children, especially in a world full of danger.

Pino and his friends listened carefully and promised to always keep an eye on the younger dino babies and help them if they got into trouble.

At the end of the day, Pino was happy that he was able to help and that he had learned something about the responsibilities and worries of parents. It was a day he would never forget.

PINO AS BABYSITTER

Pino was excited. His friends, the Dino parents, had asked him to babysit their newborn Dino children while they had important things to do. Pino felt very honored and wanted to make sure he did a good job babysitting.

The Dino parents had left him a list of instructions on how to take care of their babies. Pino read the list carefully and then made his way to the babies.

When he arrived, he saw that the dino babies were sleeping peacefully. Pino decided to be quiet so they wouldn't wake up. He played with some toys and sang soft songs to calm them down.

But suddenly he heard a loud noise from outside. It sounded like a dinosaur roar. Pino was scared and didn't know what to do. He thought about calling the dino parents, but he didn't want to disturb them unless it was something important.

Pino decided to go outside and see what was going on. He quietly snuck out of the house and looked around. That's when he saw a big dino-monster limping towards the dino-kid!

Pino was in a panic. He was afraid that the dino monster was going to attack the dino kids. He knew he had to do something to protect them.

Pino thought quickly and grabbed a piece of cloth that was lying on the ground. He ran toward the dino-monster and wildly waved the piece of cloth back and forth to scare it off.

Fortunately, it worked! The dino-monster recoiled and ran away. Pino was relieved and felt like a real hero.

When he went back into the house, the dino kids were still sleeping peacefully. Pino decided to quietly retreat and watch over them until the dino parents returned.

When the dino parents finally returned, they were so thankful that Pino had been watching their babies. They praised him for his courage and said he was a great babysitter.

Pino was happy and proud of himself. He had learned that you had to be brave to protect your friends. He knew he was ready to watch the Dino kids anytime their parents needed it.

At the end of the ride, the magical train thanked Lina for her help and promised to always take her on magical adventures. Lina was so happy and grateful for the adventure and learned that friendship and cooperation are always the keys to success.

And so Lina fell asleep with a smile on her face, dreaming of the next magical journey with her friend, the magical train.

A NIGHT OF ADVENTURE with the baby dino

Pino and his friends had a new family member: a cute baby dino named Rocco. Rocco was very curious and always wanted to explore everything. The dino's parents often had to go away to look for food, so they asked Pino to watch Rocco.

One evening, while Pino was watching Rocco, it got dark and scary in Dino Land. Suddenly they heard a strange noise. It was a loud growl that came closer. Pino looked outside and saw something he had never seen before: it was a giant T-Rex coming towards them!

Pino knew he had to protect Rocco, but he was too small to fight a T-Rex. So, he decided to run away with Rocco. They ran through the forest and hid in a cave. Pino told Rocco a story to distract him, but the growl of the T-Rex could still be heard.

Pino knew they couldn't stay in the cave forever. He thought about how he could stop the T-Rex. Suddenly he remembered that he had seen something that could stop the T-Rex: big rocks that were on a cliff.

Pino and Rocco ran to the cliff and rolled down the rocks. The T-Rex was hit by the rocks and fell to the ground. Pino and Rocco ran back to the dino nest where the dino parents were waiting for them.

The dino parents were worried when they heard about the incident, but also very proud of Pino. They explained to him that courage and creativity are important to survive in difficult situations. Pino was happy that he was able to keep Rocco and himself safe and knew that he could always rely on his strengths and abilities when he got into difficult situations.

THE DINO QUIZ

Pino and his friends were looking forward to an exciting day in Dino Land. They wanted to go on a discovery tour and learn a lot about dinosaurs. But when they got to the park, they discovered that something was different than usual. There was a big banner hung up that said, "Dino Quiz today at 3pm!".

Pino and his friends were curious and decided to participate in the quiz. They joined other children and waited for the quiz to begin. There were many questions about the different dinosaurs, their names, their characteristics and their way of life.

Pino and his friends were impressed by the knowledge of the other children and tried to learn as much as they could themselves. When the quiz started, everyone was very excited. The quizmaster asked the questions and the children had to write down the answers. Pino and his friends worked together and tried to answer all the questions correctly.

But suddenly the quiz was interrupted. A little baby dinosaur had escaped and was running around nearby. The children saw that the baby was not well and decided to help it. They caught it and brought it to the dino caretakers.

As a thank you for their help, the kids got an exclusive tour of the Dino Park and even got to see some of the dinosaurs up close. Pino and his friends were overjoyed and felt like real dino experts.

They hadn't won the quiz, but they had learned a valuable lesson. It's not always about being the best or winning the quiz. It's about working together, helping others, and learning in the process. And they had definitely accomplished that on this day.

Pino and the dino art

Pino was a little boy who was fascinated by dinosaurs. One day he decided to take a trip to the land of dinosaurs. There he met a group of dinosaurs who were all creating art. The dinosaurs were painting, carving and creating sculptures that looked so realistic as if they were alive.

Pino was so excited about the artwork that he decided to learn dinosaur art. He asked the dinosaurs if they could teach him how to create such beautiful works of art. The dinosaurs were very happy that Pino was so interested in their art and agreed to teach him how to create it.

Pino began to work hard and practiced every day. The dinosaurs taught him all about paints, brushes, and sculpting materials. Pino was so excited about dino art that he started creating his own artwork. He painted and carved and created some of the most beautiful art the dinosaurs had ever seen.

One day the dinosaurs decided to have an art show. They asked Pino to exhibit his artwork. Pino was so excited and happy that he got to show his artwork at the exhibition. When the exhibition opened, all the artworks were so beautiful and realistic that the visitors thought they were created by dinosaurs.

Pino was so proud of himself and his artwork that he decided to always stay true to dino art. He knew that through hard work and practice, he could achieve anything he wanted. Pino had learned that through persistence and passion, anything was possible.

A DAY AT THE MUSEUM

Pino and his friends were excited. Today, a trip to the museum was on the agenda. They would visit an exhibition about dinosaurs there.

When they arrived at the museum, they were amazed at the size of the building. There were people everywhere looking at the different exhibits.

The children rushed to the dinosaur exhibit. There they saw huge skeletons of T-Rex, Stegosaurus and other dinosaurs. They listened to the stories about their way of life and admired the life-size replicas of dinosaurs.

Pino was especially fascinated by the fossils. He was eager to find out how scientists were able to put the dinosaurs' bones together.

Suddenly, they heard an alarm and voices shouting through the loudspeaker, "All visitors please exit the building! There is a dangerous situation!"

Pino and his friends panicked. They looked around and noticed that some people were already running toward the exit. Pino had an idea, though. He knew that there were many hidden passages and secrets in the old dinosaur halls.

"Watch out, I know some secret passages here. Follow me!" shouted Pino to his friends.

They ran and followed Pino through a secret passage that led them to another part of the museum. As they ran through the passage, they heard strange noises.

"What is that?" a friend asked.

Pino didn't know, but they had to keep going. Finally, they came to an old door, which they opened. Behind it they saw a huge hall where strange devices were set up.

Suddenly they heard footsteps and saw that a group of thieves was approaching. They had discovered the door and were now trying to gain access to the hall.

Pino knew he had to act. He boldly stood in front of the thieves and asked them to leave the museum. The thieves just laughed and approached him.

Pino didn't know what to do, but then an idea came to him. He turned on one of the devices and it began to make a loud sound. The thieves were frightened and ran away.

The children were relieved and proud of Pino. They knew they were now safe and could leave the museum.

When they arrived outside, they were greeted by the museum staff. They thanked Pino and his friends for their bravery and offered to come back anytime.

Pino and his friends were proud of what they had accomplished. Not only had they had an exciting time at the museum, but they had also shown their courage and determination.

The visit to the paleontologist

It was a sunny day and Pino was very excited. His parents had promised him that they would visit the paleontologist today. Pino knew that paleontologists are scientists who study the fossil remains of animals and plants that lived long ago. Pino was especially interested in dinosaurs and was looking forward to learning more about them.

When they arrived at the paleontologist, they were greeted by a friendly man who showed them where they could see the different dinosaur fossils. Pino saw the huge bones and asked the paleontologist how he could figure out what kind of dinosaur it was just by looking at the bones.

The paleontologist explained that they have to do a lot of research to determine what kind of dinosaur it was. They have to consider different factors, such as the size, shape and structure of the bones, and compare them with other similar bones. They also have to study the geological layers where the fossils were found to get more information about how the dinosaurs might have lived.

Pino was very impressed with all the work it takes to gather this information and realized that paleontologists have to work really hard to find out more about dinosaurs.

Then Pino asked if he could help the paleontologist with his work. The paleontologist smiled and said, "Of course, I would have something for you to do." He gave Pino a brush and showed him how to carefully remove dust from a fossil.

Pino was very focused and began to work carefully. He was so fascinated with the work that he didn't notice how much time had passed. When he looked at the clock, he was surprised to see that it was already late and it was time to go back home.

Pino was very happy about his visit to the paleontologist. He had learned a lot about the work of paleontologists and was proud to have helped. He realized that it is important to work hard and be persistent if you want to learn or accomplish something. Pino decided to learn more about dinosaurs and maybe one day become a paleontologist himself.

PINO AS A TEACHER

Pino was a little dinosaur who always loved to learn. One day he decided to pass on his knowledge to other dinosaurs. He had many friends in his community who always listened to him when he told stories from the past. Pino thought that he could teach his friends much more if he told them about the world today.

So he decided to start a class and teach his friends. The next day, Pino called all his friends together and told them that he was going to teach them about human life. Pino had learned a lot about humans from his friend the bird and was fascinated by their inventions and way of life.

The dinosaurs were very excited and Pino started telling them about the different inventions of the humans. He explained to them how people lived in houses, how they grew food, and how they got around. The dinosaurs were very curious and asked many questions.

Pino patiently answered every question and explained everything very clearly. The dinosaurs had a lot of fun and learned something in the process. They listened attentively and asked many questions.

But then Pino noticed that one of his friends was not following along. It was Tino, a little dinosaur who was usually very attentive. Pino asked him if he had any questions. Tino sadly replied that he didn't understand much, so he couldn't ask any questions.

Pino realized that he had not focused enough on Tino. He went over to him and explained things again in a different way. Finally, Tino understood everything too and even had many questions. The other dinosaurs applauded when Tino asked his questions and they were all answered.

Pino realized that it was important to listen to each of his students and help them understand everything. He was very proud of his class and looked forward to teaching them much more.

Moral: Everyone has different abilities and needs. As a teacher or friend, it is important to be responsive to each individual and help them discover and develop their skills and strengths

THE DINO SCHOOL

Pino was a little dinosaur who lived in a time when there were no schools. One day, however, he decided it was time for the dinosaur kids to learn about the world around them.

So Pino set out to find a place where he could open a school. Finally, he found a beautiful cave near a river. There he began recording everything he knew about his world and developing a curriculum.

Soon, many dinosaur children came to Pino's school and were excited about what they were learning. Pino taught them all about plants and animals and explained how the world worked.

One day, however, Pino noticed that some of the dinosaur children were not as attentive as others. They were unfocused and inattentive and just didn't seem to understand what he was teaching them.

Pino knew he had to do something to motivate them and get their attention back. So he organized a contest where the dinosaur kids would compete against each other to test their knowledge.

The kids were excited about the idea and worked hard to prepare for the competition. When the big day finally arrived, they competed against each other and showed off their knowledge of the world around them.

At the end of the competition, there were prizes for all the participants, but Pino also made it clear that life is not only about competition and prizes, but also about being curious and learning.

The dinosaur kids left Pino's school that day with a new sense of knowledge and discovery, and Pino knew he had done something important for the dinosaur community.

Moral: Learning can be fun, but it is important to always stay curious and use knowledge to better understand the world around us.

A TEST FOR PINO

Pino was a bright little dinosaur and attended the Dino School run by Professor Triceratops. One day, the professor announced that there was an exam coming up to see which of the dino kids was ready for the next level.

Pino was excited, but also a little nervous. He knew he would have to work hard to pass. So he sat down at home and started studying. He read everything he knew about dinosaurs and asked the professor lots of questions. He showed how dedicated he was and tried to learn as much as he could.

The day of the exam finally came and all the students gathered in the classroom. Professor Triceratops started asking the questions and the students wrote down their answers. Pino found the questions harder than expected, but he didn't give up and kept going.

At the end of the exam, the professor announced the results. Some students had made it, while others had to study a little more. Pino was very nervous when he heard that his name was not on the list of students who passed.

The professor noticed how sad Pino looked and walked over to him. "Pino, I know you've been working hard," he said. "But it's okay if you didn't pass this time. The important thing is that you work hard and don't give up. You can do it next time!"

Pino was relieved and grateful for the professor's words. He decided to work even harder and prepare more intensely so that he would pass next time. He continued to study and asked the professor for advice when he didn't understand something.

When the next exam came around, Pino was ready. He was calmer than the first time and answered the questions with more confidence. At the end of the exam, his name was on the list of students who passed.

Pino was proud of himself and knew that his hard work and determination had paid off. He had learned that through hard work and determination, you can achieve your goals.

Moral: It is important to work hard and not give up if you want to achieve your goal. Mistakes and failures can happen, but it's important to learn from them and keep going to ultimately succeed.

The prom

Pino could hardly believe it, but Dino School was coming to an end. The days were flying by and it was already time for prom. Pino had been preparing for this special day for weeks. He had bought a new shirt and fancy pants and combed his spines so neatly that they almost looked like those of a real lizard.

The prom was to be held in the castle park, which was decorated with colored lights and balloons. The music was loud and happy, and all the dinos had dressed up and were dancing with each other. Pino felt a little nervous as he walked through the crowd looking for his friends.

When he finally saw them, he felt relieved. They were all there, his best friends Trino, Saura and Stego. They greeted each other warmly and immediately began to dance together. Pino was happy that he had such great friends.

But then Pino noticed that one dino was standing alone at the edge. It was the shy Ankylo, who never spoke much and was often forgotten. Pino decided to bring him over and let him join their group.

They danced together and laughed a lot. Ankylo beamed with joy, and Pino felt how proud of himself he was. Not only had he had a nice evening, but he had also helped another dino.

At the end of the evening, there was a big surprise. The principal announced that Pino and his friends were awarded as the best students. Pino felt overjoyed and proud of himself and his friends.

Later, when he went home, he thought about how important it is to help others and be there for them. He was grateful for his friends and for the wonderful time he had at Dino School. He knew he would always think back on those special experiences.

PINO SAYS GOODBYE

Pino had spent an incredible time in Dino Land and experienced many wonderful things. But now it was time to say goodbye and go back to his own world.

The Dino parents and their children were very sad to let Pino go, but they also knew it was the best thing for him. Pino had learned and experienced so much and would carry those memories with him forever.

Before he left, Pino said goodbye to all his friends. He hugged the little baby dino he had cared for for so long and gave him a kiss on the forehead. He told him that he would always take care of him, even if they could no longer be together.

Then he turned to Dino's parents and thanked them for their hospitality and for all they had taught him. They had shown him how to care for others and the importance of friendship and togetherness.

Pino promised to keep his memories of his time in Dino Land forever and to share them with others so they could learn and be inspired, too. He gave each dino friend a final kiss goodbye and then headed back to his own world.

When he arrived in his world, Pino felt a mixture of sadness and gratitude. He missed his dino friends, but he also knew that he would forever learn from them. He would always remember the importance of looking out for each other and sticking together, and he would apply those lessons to his own life.

And so ends Pino's adventure in Dino Land. But who knows, maybe someday he would return for more adventures with his beloved dino friends. Until then, he would carry his memories and lessons in his heart and be forever grateful for the time he had spent in Dino Land.

ONE LAST DAY IN DINO Land

Pino couldn't believe that his stay in Dino Land was almost over. He had experienced so much and made so many new friends that it was hard for him to say goodbye to everything. But he knew that soon he would have to return to his own world.

On his last day in Dino Land, Pino decided to enjoy every moment and experience as much as he could. He revisited all his favorite places and spent time with all his friends.

He visited the Dino Art Gallery, where he had showcased some of his own artwork, and spent time admiring his friends and praising their work. He also visited the Dino Museum, where he had learned a lot about the history of dinosaurs.

Then he met his friends at the park, where they spent the whole day playing dino games and swimming in the lake. They played tag, hide and seek, and looked for hidden dinosaur eggs.

When evening came, all the friends gathered for one last big celebration. There was music, dancing and delicious food. Pino danced and laughed and felt so happy and grateful for the wonderful time he had spent in Dino Land.

But soon it was time for Pino to say goodbye. He knew he would miss his friends and the dinosaurs, but he also knew he would be back someday.

When Pino returned to his own world, he brought with him all the precious lessons and memories he had learned in Dino Land. He knew that he would always carry a piece of Dino Land in his heart and that one day he would go on another adventure with his dino friends.

The moral of this story is that the memories and experiences we make on our travels will stay with us forever. It is important to cherish every moment and be grateful for the wonderful people and places we meet.

Impressum

LIOM LIOM
AUF DER HÖH 13A
35447 REISKIRCHEN
KONTAKT
E-MAIL: sl350sl@gmx.de

Don't miss out!

Visit the website below and you can sign up to receive emails whenever Liom Liom publishes a new book. There's no charge and no obligation.

https://books2read.com/r/B-A-AOUW-YFQGC

BOOKS 2 READ

Connecting independent readers to independent writers.

Did you love *Adventure in Dino Land*? Then you should read *Adventure on Safari*[1] by Liom Liom!

In this lovingly designed paperback, young adventurers will find a concentrated load of captivating stories from the animal world of Africa. The gripping tales transport readers into a world of exciting encounters with wild animals such as lions, elephants, giraffes, hyenas, and many more. Through the thrilling adventures and the colorful hustle and bustle in the wilderness, young readers learn about the fascinating animal world of Africa in an entertaining way. In the process, the stories not only stimulate imagination and fantasy, but also teach valuable lessons and morals such as friendship, cohesion, and overcoming fears. The handy paperback is ideal as a companion for on-the-go or as a gift for little adventurers. The gripping stories are written in language suitable for

1. https://books2read.com/u/bzKOXG

2. https://books2read.com/u/bzKOXG

children, which further enhance the reading pleasure. Immerse your children in the fascinating world of African wildlife and get them excited about the beauty and diversity of nature!